The Expat Teacher's Job Search Guide

Second Edition

By James Rogers, with Janice Seto, of

The Expat Teacher Network

Disclaimer

Even though the Author always strives for accuracy on all information in this work, the Author wishes to make it clear:

1) Due to constantly changing information, contacts, events, numbers, prices, etc, and our inability to monitor them on a day to day basis, there may be inaccurate or out-of-date information, links, etc., on any of these pages at any time.

The author claims no responsibility whatsoever as to how possible misinformation presented in any of our publications, websites or webpages may adversely affect you, your lifestyle, business or travel plans in any way.

2) The author makes no warranties or representations of any kind concerning the accuracy, suitability or safety of the information contained herein or any linked site for any purpose. Materials provided are intended for informational purposes only.

In no event shall the author, employees, agents or anyone else who has been involved in the creation, production, or delivery of these pages, be liable for any direct, incidental, or consequential damages resulting from the use of this work, site or any linked site.

The reader agrees to indemnify and hold the author from and against all claims and expenses, including attorneys' fees, arising out of the use of the book.

(Highlights of this extensively revised 2nd edition)

Introduction to the Expat Teaching Job Scene
1. Expat Teaching Jobs & Employers: What types of schools are there, and which one suits me best?
2. Stand Out for Consideration: How should I communicate with schools such that I will not be ignored?
3. Job Fairs: How can I be successful at job fairs?
4. Job Fairs: Convivial, not Cutthroat
5. Job Fairs: Recruitment Agencies: Which one(s) should I use? (new to this edition)
6. International Schools, assessing them: How can I find more information on schools I have applied to? (new to this edition)
7. Effective Job SearchTips from the Experts: What other tools do I need to be successful in my job search?

Table of Contents

Introduction to the Expat Teaching Job Scene

Don't let this happen to you! So you came to the right place to do it right.

The search for a job in an international school can be daunting to say the least. Rivers of unanswered emails and letters, multiple rejections at job fairs often from Heads of School who have, to put it diplomatically, limited people skills. This was my experience when I first ventured into the world of the expatriate teaching job hunt. The effect on your self-esteem can be intense - it was on mine. For many of us, shameless self-promotion doesn't come naturally and if our experience is limited, it is easy to feel like you've gotten in way over your head.

With this extensively-updated *2nd edition of The Expat Teacher Job Search Guide*, and this network of colleagues (The Expat Teacher Network), the hope is that we can provide some helpful assistance to colleagues who are looking to start or further their international teaching career. Teachers helping teachers.

Let's start by our definition of teacher: you are certified by some jurisdiction, probably in the West to teach children of ages ranging from K-12 in classrooms where English is the language of instruction. Whether it is Cambridge, Massachusetts or Cambridge, UK or Cambridge, Ontario, or Cambridge, Australia or Cambridge, New Zealand, where you obtained your degree and which state/province has granted your teaching certification matters a lot to get noticed by international school recruiters. They also prefer you to have subject specializations – anyone with hard sciences and math get picked over very quickly. Music and English – not so much.

A certified teacher with the added qualifications like CELTA or DELTA or other TOEFL also may attract attention but these better not be what you lead with. Like it or not, Western-certified teachers and TOEFL teachers are not courted in the same way. They teach distinctly different students and subjects.

The Expat Teacher's Job Search Guide 2nd edition will help the discerning certified teacher – it should in no way be treated as a Bible. It is as relevant as possible, although certainly incomplete and will probably contain omissions. You will see dialogue on points that some would disagree with. We can only say, it is the sum of our experience and our research. It is written in language that we hope is accessible to all. We do not sugarcoat nor are we overblunt – we know your time is valuable and you need to deal with the truth. How you handle the truth is up to you.

There are many similar documents, blogs, discussion forums and websites out there, including The International Teacher Magazine (ITM) - we know that. We freely admit, a lot of the advice we give here has come from our reading of some of these sources, or at least we can say our experience is similar and thus the information we offer is the same. So why not just direct our members to these other sources? Why not just, for example, direct our members to www.joyjobs.com which offers a comprehensive job search guide?

Frankly, because we find some of the information in many sources to be outdated. Only current information will help your cause, and help you state your case.

More importantly, many such guides present themselves as <u>advice-givers</u> rather than <u>information couriers</u>. At the Expat Teacher Network, we don't want to spend a lot of time giving you a lot of advice that may or may not be accurate or generally applicable. Rather, we want to present you with as much accurate information as possible and let <u>you make up your own mind</u>. Many of you are experienced international teachers already, and you don't need us or anyone to tell you how to construct a resumé.

Teachers who have consulted our first edition have wondered if we could add more specifics on job fairs and recruitment agencies. With that at the forefront of this second edition, we have reached *deep* to offer you information from the floor of selective job fairs and teacher recruitment agencies.

In an effort to be more succinct than many of the comparable documents that are out there, we have divided this guide into seven main sections:

1. What types of schools are there, and which one suits me best?
2. How should I communicate with schools such that I will not be ignored?
3. How can I be successful at job fairs?
4. Which job fairs should I attend?
5. Which recruitment agencies should I use?
6. How can I find out more information on the schools I have applied to?
7. What other tools do I need to be successful in my job search?

At the end of each section, there is dedicated space for you to make your own notes on what we've said/imparted in that previous section that most apply to your circumstances.

Teaching internationally, as appealing as it is professionally, isn't for everyone. Many of us have known colleagues who worked at our schools for a very brief time for a variety of reasons. What *is* true, is that the expat lifestyle and the expat teacher lifestyle can be highly addictive. Welcome to the club. If you dare to risk the addiction or if you're already addicted and you want to keep feeding your habit... keep reading.

1. Expat Teaching Jobs & Employers

Part One: What types of schools are there, and which one suits me best?

The first generalization to make about international schools is to say there is no valid generalization about international schools... well except that one. Each international school is an independent entity, with its own faculty, culture, community, host country and curriculum. If you opt to teach overseas in international schools, gone are the days where you can simply put your name in for a transfer from your current school board, change schools and preserve all of your seniority, pension and experience. Each new job at a new school is like starting over, at least in some sense.

This means that a variety of factors come into play when a teacher searches for and accepts a position overseas. School, location, teaching assignment, climate, and curriculum all play a role in deciding where you will go and which school(s) will be willing to offer you a job.

This means you really need to know yourself, not just your likes and dislikes but your real pet peeves. For example, could you survive in a country where electricity delivery and therefore internet is unreliable? Some people could, some couldn't. It doesn't matter which sort of person you are, as long as you're aware of it and it guides your job search accordingly.

A lot of the advice-givers will suggest that it is more important to target the right kind of school and not to worry about what country it's in. At Expat Teacher Network, we would respectfully disagree. If you like your school but you cannot tolerate the culture or country you are living in, for whatever reason, the experience will not be a lengthy or a positive one. Finding the right location is just as important as finding the right school.

When I first moved overseas, I worked at a "rich local kid" school (more on this terminology later) near Kuala Lumpur, Malaysia. The school was located out in the suburbs, as is often the case, and occasionally a group of us would head into "KL" to shop, and to go out to dinner (usually at the Hard Rock Café). On one occasion, we chose to take the commuter train into the city and then get a taxi downtown. Four of us piled into a taxi as we came out of the train station and told the driver the address of our destination. What followed was an approximately 20 minute discussion/debate about what the price would be. We wanted him to simply turn on the meter and charge us accordingly. He had other ideas. It was a frustrating experience to say the least. Sure, I can laugh about it *now*. Well, actually I don't laugh about it. If I think about it too much, it still irritates me, but it was something I could live with. If it was something that was beyond my tolerance zone, then regardless of school, living in Malaysia would not have been for me.

So, having said all that, what kinds of schools are out there? Which ones are better? Which ones should you pursue and which ones should you leave alone?

Categorizing overseas schools can be done in a variety of ways, depending on what you choose as your main focus. At the Expat Teacher Network, we believe schools can be put into six categories:

A. Mainstream "expat" international schools.
B. "Rich local kid" schools.
C. Overseas military schools.
D. Company-owned schools, eg. ARAMCO.
E. Proprietary schools, including private language schools, eg. SABIS, GEMS, Inlingua, QSI.
F. Religious-affiliated schools, eg. Yew Cheung International School, Hong Kong.

These are explained in detail below. Read them and decide how much these classrooms appeal to you.

A. Mainstream "expat" international school

The first type, the expat international school, are the ones we could call "real" international schools. They were established to serve the expatriate community in a particular area. They are almost always non-profit and ultimately led by a Board of Directors, which is usually composed of parents and/or representatives of the institutions which supply the students. The school I currently work at, Frankfurt International School (FIS), is a classic example of this type of school. Legally, the school is a private entity and funds the bulk of its expenses by charging tuition. In the case of schools like FIS, the tuition is usually paid by the company that employs the main breadwinner of the family, not by the family themselves.

This often means the expat students are from regular middle-class families. They are highly motivated but often not abnormally wealthy. This is usually contrasted by a percentage of the school's population that is drawn from the local community. In the case of my school (Frankfurt), these are often Germans who have previously lived overseas, thus their children's education has already been conducted in English. Parents are often demanding and expectations are high.

Such schools almost always run the International Baccalaureate (IB) curriculum (although some run the Cambridge A-Levels or the US Advanced Placement (AP). Speaking frankly, from the way things are trending, if you want to get considered, you've got to have IB training. In some cases these schools run all three sections of the IB, the Primary Years Programme (PYP), the Middle Years Programme (MYP) and the Diploma Programme (DP). Experience teaching your appropriate IB Programme will be key in securing a position at one of these schools, especially if it is located in a developed country (ie. Western Europe). With the explosion in the number of public and private schools offering the IB in the US, Canada, and the UK, this is not as difficult as it once was for North American and British teachers.

Most of these schools have some sort of accreditation, either from the Council of International Schools (CIS), some agency in the US or both. If a school doesn't, it is reasonable to ask yourself why not. If a school has had their accreditation withdrawn, this should be treated as a red flag. Passing accreditation is quite straightforward. It is not a guarantee of quality administration, but it does mean the basics are there.

When considering salary and benefits, "real" international schools vary widely, depending on their location. The Middle East and East Asia are usually the schools with the best packages. This is due mainly to a combination of low or no income tax and multiple benefits, such as free housing, annual home leave flights, relocation, free utilities etc. This is balanced by fewer public holidays and more rigorous working conditions. Such benefits are given to expat teachers for two reasons:

1. To make the school <u>more attractive</u> to prospective employees - a better package means more applicants, which in turn means a Head of School can be more choosy about whom he/she hires.
2. To <u>compensate for less desirable living</u> conditions – Face facts, if schools do not offer teachers an excellent package, they won't want to come and live on a compound in Saudi Arabia or under the polluted skies of Beijing.

Schools in Western Europe, such as Frankfurt, Brussels, Paris, the Hague, etc. offer the opportunity to live in Western Europe, which is a major drawing card for many people, but often cannot offer tax-free benefits due to restrictive tax regimes in their host country. This coupled with a higher cost of living in general means that salaries may seem high in pure mathematical terms, but often do not allow teachers to save significant amounts of money, unless you choose to live very frugally.

Schools in Southern Europe, in countries like Italy, Spain, Greece offer a great climate but often do not pay well, unless you are an administrator.

These are the most competitive schools to get hired onto, the A-List.

B. "Rich local kid" schools.

The second kind of overseas school is what we call the "rich local kid" school. These schools are definitely a cut below schools like Frankfurt IS, ISB Brussels, IS Bangkok or Nagoya International School in Japan. These second-tier schools can be misleading, as they often carry the label "international school" or "American School" but they serve primarily the wealthy local community that seeks an English-language education for their children.

One such example is the school I taught at in Guayaquil, Ecuador. It was advertised as the "American School of Guayaquil". I quickly learned the only thing American about this school was some of the teachers. The school was 98% Ecuadorian and classes were taught in both Spanish and English.

These second-tier schools are usually for profit and are mostly under the control of one person or family... with all of the positives and negatives that this implies. Profit is usually the greater motivation in these schools, so they can be frustrating at times. However, if you lack IB experience or AP experience, they are often still willing to hire you and such schools can be good places to gain experience teaching IB or AP. In some cases, they even pay for your IB training, either online or fly you to a face-to-face weekend, which will enhance your resume/CV, making you more marketable to top-drawer international schools later on.

C. The overseas military school (mainly US).

Packages here can often be very generous. Housing allowances that allow teachers to live in single-family houses in Western Europe combined with the ability to buy goods at military commissaries for much-reduced prices means teachers can usually save a good portion of their salary. I have known colleagues who stay at such schools for decades - until retirement. Often working at such schools means you exist as a quasi-diplomat, with some of the privileges and advantages that members of the foreign service receive. This can be important for those who wish to return to their home country upon retirement. If you are American and absolutely want to retire to the US or you want to be able to continue contributing to and draw from Social Security, then a DoDEA school would allow you to do this.

The downside to such schools is that are quite restrictive in their hiring. In other words, if you are not American, don't bother sending your CV to the DoDEA (Department of Defense Education Authority). They won't hire you.

Also, you cannot apply directly to the school you would want to work at. You apply to a centralized hiring authority and you are placed, maybe in a country you have no interest in living in. This is usually the case even for military schools from other countries as well. (granted, since the end of the Cold War these schools are rare). The other potentially negative aspect is the culture of these schools. The clientele of overseas military schools is usually not different from normal public (ie. state-run) schools in their home country. If you're looking to go overseas because you want a break from your country's public school system, overseas military schools will not provide this.

D. The Company School

The next type of school is the company school. Some of these schools can be *very* beneficial financially. The ARAMCO schools in Saudi Arabia are well known for their generous packages. Teachers can often save quite a lot of money working at schools like this. The downside is they are usually very business-oriented or worse, fixated on a particular educational philosophy that not all teachers will necessarily be comfortable with.

E. Proprietary Schools

A good example of this kind of proscriptive methodology is the SABIS schools, one of which is in Frankfurt, Germany. Students are tested every Friday and a teacher's employment is directly linked to the performance of your students on these tests. This school often does NOT attract the best and brightest of the Frankfurt expatriate community, so teaching here can be very frustrating. I have known one or two colleagues at my school who previously worked at this school (the International School Frankfurt Rhine Main) and are always quite happy to no longer be working there. To be fair however, if such a system of constant testing, which is the cornerstone of the SABIS system, is something you can live with, perhaps such a school would be one you could work at.

GEMS Education operates schools across the world, and once you have taught in one, it appears that you could transfer to another in their network. GEMS' network is extensive and varied however. They run thousands of schools worldwide with a wide bandwidth of quality. The top of the ladder are their "World Academy" schools which charge the most tuition, attract the best students and teachers and offer the best working conditions. It goes down the ladder from there, with their bottom-rung schools charging only a few thousand dollars in tuition and hiring only south Asian teachers whom they do not treat terribly well.

GEMS' lower-rung schools are expected to turn a profit to help subsidize their top-end schools, which run at a higher cost. The conventional wisdom on GEMS is that sometime soon, there will be financial pressure on their top-end schools to also turn a profit. Thus, working at a GEMS school for now is quite all right, but may change in the near future.

F. Religious-affiliated Schools.

Many of these schools carry the label "international school" as well and offer the IB Programme and for all intents and purposes function the same as an expat international school. The main difference is the obvious one. They will also include religious instruction and will have more specific expectations of teachers in terms of their religious beliefs and what they do with their private time.

Often compensation is also not favorable when compared to even other second-tier schools, as the assumption is you're working at the school as an expression of your commitment to the religious faith the school espouses. Jobs here are often seen as semi-volunteer work.

The advantage of this can be, jobs will be made available to new or inexperienced teachers. Sometimes even unqualified teachers can land jobs at such schools, but they receive only very basic compensation. If such restrictions are not a problem for you, then these schools can be perfectly comfortable places to work.

So, all in all, what can we at the Expat Teacher Network offer to you as a checklist that you should consider when deciding where to apply and/or where to accept a position? Keeping in mind, we don't want to be too "preachy" here or to head too much in the direction of advice-giving, we boil it down to the following items:

- **Choose a school that best fits your experience and qualifications.** If you have zero IB experience and you want to teach High School Chemistry, applying to a "top-drawer" international school like IS Prague is probably a waste of your time.
- **Don't settle for a school that is below your qualifications.** An experienced IB teacher doesn't need to take a job at a small language school teaching ESL/EFL in order to find a job overseas.

- **Choose the right school AND the right country for you.** Both are important, remember you are not just moving overseas to work, but also to live. No country nor overseas school will be right for the inflexible teacher, so examine how tolerant you are of ambiguity. Two teachers I know got work in Shanghai – one ended up at Western expat restaurants and KFC while the other ate Chinese all the time. Guess who ended up with more money in the bank? The second one is ethnic Chinese and thought she had hit the jackpot!

NOTES

2. Stand Out for Consideration

Part Two: How should I communicate with schools such that I will not be ignored?

With the advent of the internet - and particularly email - contacting schools directly has become easier than ever before. While this is a huge advantage for teachers, for schools it can be difficult and even a nightmare. Schools that are located in prime locations, ie. Western Europe, and/or schools that offer the best salary and benefit packages – the A-List – are inundated with unsolicited resumes. Top-drawer international schools can receive thousands of such inquiries per year. This has changed job searching for teachers. Now, instead of one of dozens, your CV is buried in an electronic pile that contains thousands. Well-qualified, experienced teachers can easily be overlooked purely for "needle in a haystack" reasons. So, the logical question is: how do you maximize your chances of getting a response? How do you become the needle and not the haystack?

The advice-giver websites are full of strategies for improving your chances of NOT being ignored by prospective schools. Some of the advice is good, some not. As we have already iterated, at the Expat Teacher Network, we prefer to deal in facts that are objectively verifiable rather than simply give advice that may or may not be accurate. This is not to say that what we will impart here is not the same as some of the other services out there. You can download a very comprehensive job search guide from www.joyjobs.com. A lot of the advice it contains is good. Some we would dispute. When it comes to emails, job interviews etc., we must admit, we think they've got it mostly right. So let's build a list of simple facts that can help inform you with respect to communicating with schools:

- **Job post advertisements are notoriously unreliable.** At my own school, I have seen multiple postings over the years for a job that everyone at the school knew was going to go to a specific internal candidate. But, under German law and our Collective Bargaining Agreement, the school cannot simply award the job to that person, it must be advertised. Be aware of this. It doesn't mean you should not send that school an email, but be aware of one simple truth: many jobs awarded in international schools are never advertised - my current position wasn't.

- **Shorter Emails that ask ONE simple question get answered more often, longer Emails don't.** The folks at JoyJobs say that a good rule of thumb is to keep Emails to a maximum of 250 words.[1] We think that's a good piece of advice. Emails that are likely to get a response are those that are succinct, direct and that ask for action. In other words, pose a question, not two, that requires the school to respond to you. An example would be, "I was visiting your website and you clearly have a top-notch school. I am curious if you offer IB Higher Level classes separately from Standard Level or are they mixed?"

---

[1] Pamela Campbell and Igor Smirnov, The Job Guide: An Inside Approach to Recruitment, p. 49.

- **Don't be afraid to send Emails to schools that don't advertise a specific vacancy in your area.** Job openings can happen rather spontaneously. Someone has to return to their home country because of family issues, someone gets offered a "better" job out of the blue, someone's health takes a bad turn. The reasons are numerous and varied. What this means is schools will often have openings that never get advertised. Why? Because the opening occurs without warning, and that school has your resume on file, because you sent them an Email several weeks ago, and they call you, interview you and hire you. The point is: don't assume no advertised vacancy means no job in your area.

- **Use your subject area as the Email subject.** We admit, we swiped this right out of the JoyJobs Guide.[2] It's just simple logic. If you send an Email with a subject line that says: IB Chemistry teacher with IB Examiner Experience, this is much more likely to cause an administrator to open that email. If he/she is looking for a Chemistry teacher, or thinks they might need one in the near future, they'll spend the few moments (assuming your Email isn't too long) reading your message and because you've asked a question, they'll be more likely to respond. This means your foot is in the door.

- **Send your CV as an attachment.** This is also just common sense. What has changed in the past 10 years is the length. It used to be, CVs for international teachers could be pages upon pages and Heads of School didn't mind. Now they do. Keep it brief, <u>maximum two pages</u> is a good rule of thumb. Also, don't forget to send the file with your name as part of the file name title. Simply sending a PDF titled "My Resume" runs the risk of becoming part of the haystack.

- **Do your homework first.** By this, we mean you need to make sure you double-check the Email address you're sending your message and CV to. Email addresses can become obsolete. Also, perhaps the Head of School doesn't pay attention to your message, but the appropriate Principal will. Always check and don't be afraid to send your message to multiple people using the blind copy function (Bcc) in your email software.

- **If you get a response, follow up with another message.** If you send an Email, get a response and then don't do anything after that, it's easy for the school to believe you've lost interest and are pursuing other opportunities. So, the best way to indicate continued interest is to write another message, ask another question and state directly that you are still interested in the job.

- **Don't be afraid to employ the tactics of Troy.** O.K. actually the Trojan Horse was used by the Greeks *against* the Trojans, but that doesn't rhyme! This idea sounds confusing, so let us explain.

You send an email to a Head of School asking your question relating to a specific opening. He/she writes back and tells you the opening is no longer open or that they don't consider your CV to be what they're looking for. Many

---

[2] ibid. p. 47.

13

people will not bother to respond to such Emails and think, "oh well, so much for that school then." But it can be an opportunity. Write a short Email back to that Head of School and ask them if they're aware of other schools in their country/area that might be hiring or interested in someone like you. (Fact: expat administrators all seem to know each other.)

Sometimes you'll get the "I don't know and don't bug me with nonsense like this" reply. Other times, you'll get a response with the name of a school or Head of School. This becomes the lead sentence to your Email when you contact that second school. "Dr. So-and-So from the International School of Such-and-Such suggested I contact you..." The chances the Director of this second school will keep reading are higher. Again, your foot is now in the door.

- **Don't sound desperate or ambivalent.** The truth is, no school will hire you if they think you're desperate (it begs the question, why will no one else hire you?) or if they think you're just "window shopping" as some of the advice-giver websites put it. Sound confident but not arrogant. This is the key to maintaining or securing your status as the needle and not the haystack.

Ultimately the goal is to gain recognition, and arrange either a Skype interview (much more common these days) or an interview at an upcoming job fair that both you and the school will be attending. If you can manage this, you're well on your way to securing a position.

But at all times remember the two watch words: BE WARY, BE SKEPTICAL. A school that is turned off by someone wanting to know more, is no school you should want to work at. With this is mind, you could head off to a teaching job fair and really slug it out in the trenches. In the next section, we deal specifically with job fairs, as these are still one of the major tools used by international schools to hire. With the advent of Skype, it's possible this will change, but for now, job fairs are still an important part of the hiring process.

NOTES

3. <u>Job Fairs</u>: How can I be successful at job fairs?

Part Three: How can I be successful at job fairs?

If you've never taught overseas before, or your teacher's college did not organize one, you might not even know what a job fair is. You graduated from Teacher's College, applied to various school districts, landed an interview, got hired, and voilà, you had a career! Experienced expatriate teachers know that for international schools, it doesn't work this way.

One of the still-used tools of recruitment for overseas schools is the job fair. They are daunting, humbling events that can leave you feeling like a not-so-prized heifer at a cattle market. Having said that, if you want to move jobs in the international school circuit or if you are trying to break into this circuit for the first time, you'll almost certainly need to attend at least one job fair. This begs the question: which job fair should you attend? Should you even attend a job fair at all?

As with the other parts of this guide, there are a slew of advice-giver websites out there that will tell you all sorts of things about job fairs. Some of the advice is accurate, some frankly doesn't match our experiences here at the Expat Teacher Network. Granted, individual experience may not be typical, so as always, we'll try to stick to objective factual information here.

Let's start with the most basic of job fair-related questions: is it still necessary to attend a job fair? Do schools still value them? While it's true that the advent of Skype has almost made job fairs for international schools unnecessary, that face-to-face contact is still valued to some degree and it is advantageous for both sides. Direct personal contact is still the most informative way for schools to assess candidates and for candidates to assess schools. Certainly, my school (Frankfurt) still attends at least one job fair every year. Granted, they used to attend three or four during the recruiting season that starts November/December and usually lasts til March, so the trend is obvious.

Janice, my co-author, offers this insight: job fairs benefit you the teacher/job-hunter as much as the recruiting school.

The whole point of a job fair for the recruiter is to meet a bunch of teachers, shortlist a smaller number to interview, then decide if one fits what they want and ultimately offer someone job - with the caveat to accept within a few days, if not a few hours.

For you the expat teacher, you are there for the long game of your teaching career, not just for a job. You get to size up a range of schools from any number of presentations or meet-and-greets. Plus, you get to meet other teachers and start building a network. Think of it as an investment in your career.

There are a variety of job fairs run by various agencies and universities. We cover the various job fairs and the pluses and minuses of each later on. So for now, let's assume you've found the job fair you wish to attend and we'll stick to discussing what you need to do to increase your chances of securing interviews and job offers.

Job fairs can be broken down into two types, selective and non-selective.

a. <u>Selective</u> simply means the organizers of the fair will only allow you to attend if you meet their minimum qualification requirements. This ensures to their attending schools that the pool of available candidates will be ones that are not a waste of their time and have a reasonable chance of securing interviews and job offers. Generally speaking, the minimum is teaching certification and two years of experience. Obviously more-than-the-minimum is better - more on this later.

b. <u>Non-Selective Job Fairs</u> basically admit anyone, because the more who buy their way in, the more money the job fair organizers make. The selectives keep their numbers manageable whereas non-selectives will sell tickets to anyone willing to pay the price of admission so you get a mix of fresh-grads and experienced international teachers.

The other key factor to remember with job fairs is that the recruiters themselves can be broken down into two basic categories, those that are <u>serious</u> and don't mind the recruitment trail, and those that <u>hate it</u> and would rather be anywhere else. I remember attending the ECIS (now CIS) Recruitment Fair in London one January and going to an interview with a very personable, pleasant principal. I could easily have envisioned myself working for him... in theory. Throughout the whole interview, held in his hotel room (the norm at these job fairs), he kept the television on to watch the soccer (read football if you're not North American) match. It was pretty obvious that he wasn't serious about recruiting, or at least not serious about recruiting me.

Janice adds another important fact: your immediate goal in the job fair is get shortlisted for interviews. In the old days before the internet and email, the recruiters would arrive a couple days ahead of the job fair and get their hands on massive binders from the organizers. In these binders will be dossiers on each of the job-seeking teachers. Recruiters would stay up late identifying who they wanted to shortlist although some had a strategy of wait-and-see... Like club signup at high school, the job fair usually sets up a massive hall where each recruiting school gets a desk and a sheet for interview slots for the entire job fair. Teachers line up at the desks of schools asking the recruiter for a coveted interview slot. Like a dance card in a Victoria novel, a small subset of recruiters waits and sees who shows up – and when all the slots of filled, latecomers are SOL.

<u>Given the aforementioned reality from Janice, I can share with you that The real key to success at job fairs</u> is to arrange your interviews via Email <u>ahead of time</u>. If they can block out a time to interview you before the job fair is even open, you enter the scrum with an ace-in-the-hole - and that does wonders for your confidence. Don't forget even the most serious recruiters often have a grueling schedule of interviews spread across time zones and continents to the point where they are usually receptive to anything that makes the whole process easier for them.

What's also true is that the sign-up procedure at job fairs can be chaotic to say the least. Dozens of schools sitting behind desks with seemingly unending lines of prospective candidates all waiting to charm them into granting an interview. Needless to say, a little shameless self-promotion goes a long way in such circumstances. Of course there are those schools from the less-desirable parts of the world where the Director is often sitting there hoping that anyone who passes by will stop and talk. If you remain flexible about where you go, these schools can be good opportunities. Given that the school of your dreams may not find you a good fit and decline the opportunity to offer you a job, focus on filling up your time at the job fair by getting to know schools that are not 'flavour of the month'. There might be something – you never know til you take the initiative.

Tales from the Scrum of a Job Fair (I did it so you can read about it)
The best way to impart information about what job fairs are like is to share a few facts from my own personal experience. You get a lot of text on the advice-giver websites about how one should go about landing interviews and jobs at these job fairs. As always, the advice is mixed in terms of its accuracy and helpfulness. One thing is undeniably true: recruiters will grant interviews to people primarily based on their experience and qualifications. After all, if they haven't met you yet, they can't possibly appreciate the magnetism of your wonderful personality. A few facts seem to be objectively true.

1. Scope out the Schools. You need to have your own plan of attack. Many of the advice-giver websites call this "guerrilla tactics" by which they mean choosing and planning where and when to strike. Put simply: you need to know which schools you want to approach. You need to have contacted these schools beforehand. You need to approach these schools in order of *your* preference.
   Janice put it to me this way, "you have done this before, strategizing the buffet, you do not fill up on bread… Most job fairs will have a password-controlled webpage for registrants to check out which schools will be there, which positions they are currently hiring for, compensation and overview."

2. Cut to the Chase of Who You Are. You need to approach recruiters with a confident but not arrogant attitude and lead with your most positive asset. At a recent (2016) Search Associates Job Fair, I always approached recruiter desks by saying, "I see you have a history vacancy. Would you be interested in talking to someone who has 18 years of IB experience?". To be frank, it's rare that any recruiter will say no to this. After all, someone with a lot of relevant experience is at least worth talking to, right? I managed to score 6 interviews on the first day at a job fair that had only 8 or 9 history openings. I was exhausted by the end of it all, to say the least

3. Your CV is Your Calling Card. The method of communication for your experience and qualification is your CV and/or your website. (CV is used in the overseas schools scene more often than the term 'resume'.) Which CVs do recruiters see? Those of all the teachers attending the fair. So, this leads me to my own story once again.

In 1998 I attended my first job fair. Typical of people who are unaware, I chose to attend the ECIS (now CIS) recruitment fair held in London in January. I knew it was the premier teaching job fair in the world. As I was living in Kuala Lumpur at the time, that meant a thirteen hour, fifty minute flight each way. I went home from this fair with nothing to show for it, having had very few interviews, meaning the cost of the hotel and flight seemed ludicrous.

Why wasn't I successful? I had no IB experience and had only been teaching overseas for a couple of years. Most of the other candidates at the fair had years, even decades, of IB experience and had been overseas for more than ten years. No wonder I disembarked with nothing to show for my time at ECIS.

Fast forward to the Queen's University Teachers Overseas Recruiting Fair (TORF), Canada in February 2000. Just two years after ECIS handed me my butt on a plate... By this time I had a little IB experience thanks to my job in Ecuador, and I had been overseas for a total of three or four years. Most of the other candidates at the fair had never been overseas and few had any IB experience. I had twelve interviews in two days. I was completely exhausted. I also had one job offer during the fair, and another one in my Email inbox on Monday morning. Definitely a different experience!

While it might seem reasonable to argue my experience was so different because I had a little more experience and had some IB experience under my belt, I would dispute this to an extent. True, I had more of the right kinds of experience, but my IB experience was very limited and I had only been teaching for about one to two years more at this point.

Here's the key: **The real difference was my CV vs. the CV of other candidates at the fair.** In other words, I looked good compared to the competition - and those Directors had come to hire, not to browse.

It also had little to do with my interview skills. The job offer I got by Email, I remember very well. The only thing I said during the entire interview was, "Hi, my name is Jim Rogers". He did all the rest of the talking. Needless to say, all the alarm bells were ringing in my head by the end of that interview. Why doesn't he want to ask me anything? Why doesn't he want me asking him anything? Conclusion: keep looking.

It can be similar but with a very different outcome. At the 2016 Search Associates Fair, I interviewed with a school in Riyadh, Saudi Arabia – it must be said, not an A-List school – the recruiter's first words were: "is there anything you'd like to ask us?". I remember a telling feeling in the pit of my stomach – isn't *he* supposed to ask *me* some questions first? I spent an hour with this school and never heard from them again. I wasn't disappointed.

4. You Gotta Bring It. According to Janice, another advantage of the face-to-face job fair over a Skype interview throws us shyer teachers a bone. We can be there and we can bring it, in other words, we can let our brag sheets ie student work, photos tell a thousand words on our behalf to the recruiter.

We've had a look at various advice-giver sources and boiled it all down into a bullet list of things to do to maximize your chances. Keep in mind, all of this depends on any person's ability to interview well and to have decent qualifications and experience. If you're horrible at interviewing, this will be a handicap for you regardless of how good your CV looks. On the other hand, without an attractive CV (ie. without the qualifications and experience) you won't even get an interview. Insofar as we can figure, the magic list is <u>the magnificent seven</u>.

- **Make and bring a teaching portfolio.** This is often a small binder with hard copies of some of your other paperwork, for example teacher certificates, university transcripts, evaluation reports from past administrators, as well as photos of you "in action" teaching your class. Such portfolios are a strong indication to Directors that <u>you take your teaching seriously</u> as well as your job search. It's a sign you're prepared.

  These are less useful and less in demand than they used to be, but making one isn't terribly time-consuming and if you don't end up needing it, you're no worse off. It can however, be a great and easy way to introduce a recruiter to your teaching as well as a convenient way to carry around your CV and other documents (university transcripts for example) that might be needed if you get an offer. Having them handy makes it clear you're serious and well-prepared.

- **Stay in the same hotel as the conference.** This isn't a must, especially if doing so is beyond your budget. Perhaps you could even find it desirable to have a "sanctuary" that is away from the fair. Some of these job fairs (Search Associates London) are held in expensive hotels but there is a distinct advantage to being in the same hotel as the Directors. You are more available, you can take breaks in between interviews more easily, and you do not have to be constantly commuting back and forth every day. If they text asking if you are available to interview in 45 minutes, and you are just down the hall, the answer is hell-ya!

  Also, nearby can have an additional downside. At my most recent job fair experience, I stayed at a small hotel just a few doors down the road from the job fair hotel. I paid a lot of money for a tiny room at a hotel that had a lousy breakfast buffet. By contrast, a colleague (actually a former roommate I hadn't seen in 20 years, one of the other fringe benefits of job fairs.) stayed at a nearby Holiday Inn, which offered her a wonderful breakfast buffet and a much more spacious room. Needless to say, I didn't feel too intelligent. Of course, if the self-catering route is to your taste, these days, there are always a multitude of private apartments or rooms available on the internet, usually through www.airbnb.com.

- **Look professional, dress appropriately.** Sounds like just common sense right? You'd be amazed at what people will wear to interviews. Dress professionally if you want to land a job offer. To do otherwise indicates not only a lack of professionalism but a lack of interest.

- **Have a plan of attack.** Make a list of schools in order of YOUR preference. Seek these schools out first at the sign-up sessions. Schools like knowing they're number one on your list. After all, who doesn't want to be someone else's first choice? How would you react if you knew a school hired you with a "oh I guess you'll have to do" attitude?

- **Make a good impression.** Be confident, not arrogant. Don't talk too fast, don't talk too much, give a firm handshake. Project an image that's the truth: you are an experienced, highly-capable teacher who would be a very positive addition to any school. Above all else, be honest! Don't try to talk your way around a tough question. Recruiters will spot this and will not think well of you for it.

- **Don't bad mouth current or former schools.** This is the one very strict exception to what we just said. If asked about your current or former school, focus on the positive. If this isn't possible, then you need to lie or steer the question to another topic. Some Directors will lay this trap on purpose. They're looking to avoid hiring people that they believe are going to cause trouble.

- **Be aware that every year is different with different trends.** Each new recruiting season brings with it its own demands and supplies. In casual conversation, my principal spoke of attending a job fair in recent years needing to hire a math teacher. She found it difficult as there were very few math teachers at the fair. By the time the following year came around, she needed a math teacher again and was overwhelmed with CVs.

  A distinct trend I noticed during a recent hiring season is schools that offer free housing were focused very deliberately on hiring teaching couples to reduce expenses. One recruiter even told me his Board of Directors had informed him he was authorized to hire only couples for this very reason. Every year is different and it can be that your search is happening in a year that is not terribly compatible with the trends. This was certainly the case for me in 2016. There were very few IB History jobs available. Consider being flexible about the kind of job you're willing to take and/or interview for.

That's our take on job fairs, in as succinct a manner as we can. As with other sections of this document, we know there are other organizations out there that provide much more comprehensive and detailed advice. Some of this advice is good, some not so good. Our goal at the Expat Teacher Network is to not overwhelm members with information, but to provide a manageable amount of information without being too "this is what you should do".

Let's move on now to a comparison of the top job fairs and different recruitment agencies that are necessary for securing a job in international schools these days. Some will be pro-active and helpful, some not. However, without them, you do yourself a great disservice.

NOTES

4. Job Fairs: Convivial, Not Cutthroat

Part Four: The Convivial Job Fairs

So, let's move on and have a look at the various job fairs on offer and give you some information that will help you decide which one is best for you. The job fairs tend to be run by either universities or recruiting agencies. The latter include agencies, like CIS, International School Services (ISS) and the Search Associates fair and are large and are there to make everyone happy – teachers, schools, profit margins. The ones run by universities usually are just happy to break even because their purpose includes giving their graduates, who tend to have slim CVs, a chance to get work with a modest registration fee. With that goal in mind, it is not in their best interest to run a high-stress, cutthroat fair. Rather, these are rather convivial.

The fairs at UNI (University of Northern Iowa) and the Queen's TORF (Queen's University, Kingston, Ontario) are easier in the sense that often they will take people who don't have as much experience and the schools there are a mixture of top-drawer schools and second-tier schools, such that landing a job for younger, less experienced teachers is still very possible.

As we've previously said, the big recruiting agencies host fairs that look and feel like cattle markets. They are intimidating and can be overwhelming, especially if you're naturally a shy person. If this is you, think long and hard before registering for these fairs. If the experience is going to be horrible for you, and you'll be nervous the whole time, including in interviews, you're better off staying home. With Skype, recruitment directly by the school is always a possibility.

What's also true to say is, the more experienced (especially with the IB) you are, the less likely it is you'll even need a job fair. A colleague of mine was recently hired by an excellent A-List school based solely on two Skype interviews. He received his job offer on October 9th! He is in his mid-30s with several years of IB experience, plus he has a solid record of coaching and even some administrative experience. He is obviously a top candidate. Is his new school going to risk him still being available by the time a random job fair rolls around? – NO!!!

Of course, if your paperwork (ie. experience and qualifications) look good, then a big-time job fair will probably not be a negative experience at all.

Whether you opt for a recruiting agency fair or a university-run fair, what seems to be objectively true is that you need to have a thick skin. Regardless of your experience and qualifications, at least one school is likely to say no, either before or after the interview. Janice correctly says that this is a numbers game, and in the end, all you need is one good offer.

My most recent job fair experience saw a school leave a note in my file saying that, "at this point in our school's development, we are opting for enthusiasm over experience." Needless to say, I was not at all disappointed to be rejected by a school that communicates in such an unprofessional manner. Generally speaking, rejection is something we all find disappointing and patience can be the hardest virtue to own.

Here at the <u>Expat Teacher Network</u>, we put it this simply: don't despair, don't be desperate.

All of these things, we at the Expat Teacher Network have learned via one of the great unspoken benefits of job fairs: **personal networking in the candidate lounge.**

In this section, we look at two of the most well-known convivial teacher job fairs. They charge relatively low registration fees and are definitely off the beaten path in terms of access to international airports. Warning: Both fairs are held once a year in the deepest winter of January/February so wear a parka!

a. **UNI – University of Northern Iowa**
   www.uni.edu/placement/overseas/

Our first stop on this journey is the massive job fair held by the University of Northern Iowa. UNI (and ISS) runs a non-selective fair that is massive in size and contains a large mixture of experienced and newly-qualified teachers. So, the advantages and disadvantages are generally exactly the same as with ISS.

They have an "all-in" registration fee of **US$50**. Comparatively, this is a bargain! This fee allows you to register for free for the UNI fair, it allows you access to their job database and access to "Support Staff and Publications" (their words, not ours). I admit I have never registered with UNI, so I cannot speak to their exact meaning of these last terms. Other similarities to ISS include no placement fees but also no direct assistance as you would get at a Search Associates fair. Ya gets what ya pays for.

The teaching job fair is always held in Ames, Iowa at the UNI campus. The advantage to this is the less expensive hotel costs as compared to say a London or Dubai fair. What is also true however is that getting to Ames can be expensive. Ames is a smaller city, with no international airport. Candidates need to fly to Des Moines and then make their own way to Ames, which could involve renting a car or an expensive taxi ride.

Another disadvantage to the UNI fair is that because it is in February and the other recruitment agencies hold their fairs in January, coupled with its massive size, means many schools who register for the fair will cancel before it actually takes place. Why? Because they would have filled their future teaching needs earlier in the recruitment season.

What seems to be a growing trend, is international schools demand resignations earlier and earlier in the academic year, so that they can recruit with "definite" positions as opposed to "tentative" which can cost them the chance at the best candidates. This makes it difficult. If you've been made to give notice by November 15th and the job fair is in January, you'll be much more likely to accept the first offer that comes your way.

I witnessed this when I attended the Search Associates London fair one January (2016). I could see a level of desperation amongst a lot of candidates that would do them no favours if it were conveyed in an interview. One young couple I know at this same fair, took a job in Dubai after being in Qatar for years. They were not really interested in staying in the Middle East, and the school they landed at is not an A-List school by any stretch, but it was their first offer and they needed a job. They had been forced to resign from their school in Qatar by December 1st.

In 2016 the Anglo-American School of Moscow, Frankfurt International School, the American School of Bombay, and IS Panama all cancelled in the two weeks leading up to the UNI fair. These are all A-List schools. Obviously for candidates this could be incredibly frustrating if you've registered for the UNI fair hoping to make contact and interview with one of these schools.

Also, the large number of newly-qualified teachers means many A-List schools, like my school in Frankfurt, prefer to avoid the UNI fair for the same reasons we mentioned in the subsection about ISS: too many underqualified candidates makes it difficult to sift through all the CVs to find people you *actually* want to interview.

From a technical perspective UNI's website seems to be quite user-friendly and free from technical hitches.

b. **Queen's University Teachers' Overseas Recruitment Fair (TORF)**
   http://educ.queensu.ca/torf

For Canadians starting off or mid-career or curious about international teaching, TORF is the job fair of The Great White North. The smaller "Teachers' Overseas Recruitment Fair" or TORF is held every January/February at the Faculty of Education at Queen's University in Kingston, Ontario, Canada. Like UNI and ISS, TORF attracts a mixture of newly-qualified and experienced teachers. In fact, because it is sponsored by the Faculty of Education at Queen's University (the Canadian one, not the one in Belfast) it always reserves spaces at its fair for newly-qualified teachers. These teachers obviously have a much narrower field of choice in terms of vacancies, quite a number focused mainly on intern positions.

*** Search Associates also offers assistance to "teacher interns" – a way for newly-qualified teachers to break into the international teaching circuit – but be aware compensation is very limited and can often not be enough to live on. At my school, most "interns" work as teacher assistants. They have a proper pay scale and can be members of our union and their salaries are negotiated along with the regular faculty. However, the compensation is such that these positions are mainly held by so-called "trailing spouses" (this is international school code for the non-teaching spouse of a faculty member). Thus their income is a supplement and not the main income of the family.***

Because TORF charges a modest registration fee to recruiters as well as teachers, a few A-List schools recruit there, more than you would expect. The lower Canadian dollar might have something to do with it. Because TORF is usually held before UNI, some schools fill their teaching needs at Queen's and then cancel at UNI.

Most teachers that attend TORF are Canadians and a large number are Ontario-qualified though teachers have come from as far as Alberta. Also, a much greater percentage of the schools that attend TORF are those international schools that are running a Canadian curriculum. This means that the schools recruiting there can really vary in quality. Candidates will be met by recruiters from as diverse a quality bandwidth as IS Brussels – definitely an A-List school - to the Maple Leaf Schools, many of which are in China and offer a very different working experience. This also means schools are a mixture of IB curriculum and non-IB (usually Canadian curriculum of some sort and AP) schools. A few are both, such as the Canadian International School of Singapore. This reflects the growing number of schools offering IB in Canada itself.

If you examine TORF's list of attending schools from previous years, you'll notice that most schools are B or C-List schools. This does mean however that teachers with less IB and little or no overseas experience stand a good chance of landing interviews and job offers.

Not to be overlooked by teachers, TORF does not stand for tomfoolery by recruiting schools when it comes to breaking contracts with teachers. Rumour has it that these schools were not allowed back to Queen's TORF.

TORF is a long-established fair. It operated in Canada for many years pretty free from competition for international teachers. However, the introduction of the Search Associates Toronto fair, held in early December, this is no longer the case.

Search Toronto undoubtedly attracts the candidates with more international and IB experience. But then again, Search Associates require more paperwork than TORF. If you are based in Canada, the good news for you is that you have more choice than previously and you can focus your efforts on the fair that suits you and your experience best. In terms of school location, both the Search Toronto fair and TORF tend to attract a lot of schools from Latin America, the Caribbean and eastern Asia.

Due to subsidies from the Queen's University Faculty of Education, TORF's fees are cheaper than other recruitment fairs, costing around only **C$125**. Candidates can also register or opt to avail themselves of the "online services only" option, where you do not attend the fair, but have access to the jobs database. TORF's database in our experience is significantly more limited than say Search as it is not as well-known or as well-used as the bigger recruitment agencies.

Candidates to TORF also now have the option of registering with CIS as the two agencies have formed a working partnership of some sort. You will be given access to the CIS jobs database, provided you are willing to go through with the registration process at CIS. The two agencies still exist relatively independently of each other, but the connection can be convenient for teachers, especially if they are new to the international teaching experience. Please do keep in mind our information about CIS presented in this booklet though, specifically the advantages and disadvantages of dealing with CIS.

The final two things to say about TORF are that they hold only one fair a year, like UNI and it is usually in late January or early February. Kingston, Ontario is a lovely small university town in eastern Ontario, about 3 hours east of Toronto, 4 hours west of Montreal, and where hotel and restaurant prices will be significantly cheaper than London, Bangkok, San Francisco, Dubai or any of the other normal recruitment fair locations. Of course Canada in winter is also not necessarily for the faint of heart, if you don't deal well with cold weather. ☺ At the same time, the atmosphere at TORF is supportive, positive, and convivial – if you want to dip your toe into international teaching, it is a good way to check it out.

NOTES

5. <u>Job Fairs</u>: <u>Recruitment Agencies</u>: Which one(s) should I use?

PART FIVE: Job Fairs: Recruitment Agencies: which one(s) should I use?

A lot of what we are going to say I this section might seem a bit repetitive and redundant because the major job fairs are run by the big recruitment agencies. However, given that it is possible to find a job without a job fair, we felt we needed to focus separately on the various head-hunting agencies, as we feel that there is information you need to know. In order to do that, we're going to break this section down into distinct subsections that deal with each of the major agencies. Again, our goal is not to provide advice so much as it is to impart factual, objective information and allow you to make up your own mind. We'll start with the more well-known agencies and then move to the perhaps less-obvious ones.

As a general rule of thumb, the CIS fairs and the one large Search Associates fair in London, England are the hardest nuts to crack. If you have no overseas experience and/or no IB experience, as I learnt, these fairs will basically be a waste of your time and money. The other Search Associates fairs are smaller, friendlier and more manageable. You'll probably find that schools are much more willing to interview you, even if they believe they won't hire you. The reason for this is simple: the number of candidates at the fair is limited such that Directors have time to fit you in. At the big fairs like CIS, they don't because they need to reserve those interview spots for candidates that they believe are the strongest.

<u>The key is learning to read the signals that recruiters give out</u>. Many years ago, when I attended the CIS (then ECIS) fair in London (1998), I was granted interviews on the second and third day of interviewing. I was happy and thought I had made a positive impression. I was mistaken.

Years later, when I attended a Search Associates Fair having over 20 years of teaching experience and over 18 years of IB experience, I noticed a difference. First of all, nearly every school said yes to my request for an interview and they all *insisted* that I be interviewed on the first day. I quickly realized, day two and three were going to be used for the "call back" interviews. This is something I had not known at my last job fair. I received "call back" requests, but from schools that were definitely worse (ie. not A-List) than mine. I chose to say thanks but no thanks and stay where I was and look again the following year. A luxury I had as I had not been made to resign in advance of the fair.

c. **Search Associates**
www.searchassociates.com

Search Associates has become the premier and largest international/overseas school teacher recruitment agency. We at the Expat Teacher Network openly admit that we have used and been registered candidates with 'Search' off and on since

1998. Search Associates is arguably the only truly international recruitment agency available to teachers. The senior associates (Janice would say they are like acting talent agents) include experienced educators from the US, Great Britain, Canada, Australia, New Zealand and many other countries. In all cases, these senior associates have lived and worked all over the world. Sometimes their advice can be a bit out of date, but usually it's accurate in our experience. That is why they are now the 'go-to' agency for A-List schools – recruiters get a pre-screened selection of teachers.

Search Associates is also more selective than others (at least in theory) about who they take on as a candidate. You have to qualify to be on the Search Associates teacher roster – and substantial documentation of your experience to back you up. Basically, teachers looking for jobs via Search have to be screened in. You will be required to have an interview with your Senior Associate before you can officially be invited to join their roster – at least this used to be the case.

Sometimes in the past, people have been rejected, because Search did not feel they would be sufficiently able to find a job. The reasons for this can be varied, ie. a teacher with a non-teaching spouse. A lot of these "rules" have been relaxed over the years, as the schools themselves have loosened up on their hiring protocols. For example, in 1998, the schools in Saudi Arabia would only interview and hire couples. This is no longer true. What we can say objectively, is that there doesn't seem to be any specific group or demographic that does better with Search Associates and their job fairs.

The chief benefits for teachers on the Search Associates roster compared to other agencies is the level of personal service and advice you will be given/have access to. Probably the best example of this is Search's practice of assigning each teacher at a job fair to a senior associate. This senior associate will be available in their hotel room at the fair pretty much the entire time the fair is running. Any of their assigned candidates (teachers or administrators) is welcome to drop by and chat with them about a particular school, job offer, interview or anything that is on their mind. It can give you the feeling of having your own agent, much like a Hollywood actor – though in my case without the good looks and multimillion dollar film deal.

This was not always the case. When I attended a Search Associates Fair in Oxford in 1998, this service was not available, though the fair was small and the organizers certainly made themselves available as much as they possibly could.

Even outside of job fairs, your senior associate can be helpful. In 1998, when I was looking for a job, I had sent out many CVs only to be ignored, including by the American School of Guayaquil. In a moment of frustration, I sent an email to my Search senior associate, to ask him what I was doing wrong. He suggested I allow him to contact the school directly on my behalf. To make a short story even shorter, the American School of Guayaquil contacted me within 24 hours and within 72 hours I had a new job. If I skip ahead to 2000, my current job in Frankfurt, as I've mentioned earlier, was never advertised anywhere. How did my school make contact with me? By going through Search Associates.

Search Associates has also become the main go-to agency for candidates and schools for job fairs. They operate 13 separate job fairs during the recruiting season, running from November to June. These fairs are held all over the world, such that attending one should be within your budget regardless of where you live. Whether London, Toronto, Dubai or Bangkok is easiest, there will be a fair for you.

What's also necessary to mention however is that not all of the same schools attend all the fairs. Obviously, the fair in Dubai for example tends to attract more schools from the Middle East than say the Boston or San Francisco fairs.

Sadly, our research has found one very depressing exception to this that we at the Expat Teacher Network don't believe to be the fault of Search Associates. In our research, we discovered blog and newsletter entries that were written by colleagues who were of non-European (non-Western) decent. They spoke of a very different experience at job fairs in general, not just ones run by Search Associates, though their examples were based on their experience at a Search fair. They spoke of latent racism when it came to hiring, especially among schools from the Middle East and Asia. These schools were not terribly willing to hire teachers of non-European descent, as they would often receive negative reactions from their parent community. It must be said, we at the Expat Teacher Network have not experienced this ourselves, nor witnessed this at job fairs we've attended. Also, this comment was describing what we have termed as "rich local kid" schools and not A-List schools.

Moving on to less unpleasant topics, let's deal with some hard facts about Search Associates that will allow you to compare them to the other agencies. Their fairs are by invitation only – as we have already mentioned – and this in theory means that both candidates and schools are "vetted". As a candidate this means you can be assured that the schools attending are at least of a minimum quality. Our experience at the Expat Teacher Network is that this is highly theoretical. Many schools at Search Associates fairs are not A-List schools. This is where personal networking (and information booklets like ours) become important. Search has expanded its business greatly in the past 10 years. Of course, this all depends on your experience and qualifications. Maybe you're a newly qualified teacher or you have no overseas or IB experience such that an A-List school is probably not a reasonable goal.

From the school side, this "vetting" means they can be assured that the candidates they interview at the fair are all of a minimum quality as well. You must be an "active" candidate with Search Associates to attend a fair and you must request an invitation. Don't wait for Search to ask you, they won't. Requesting these invitations and seeing the overview of which fairs are available is very easy. Search's website is quite user-friendly, easy to navigate and we personally have not experienced any technical issues with it.

Search Associates, like all of the recruitment agencies, charges a fee and requires you to submit various documents to join their organization. Search's documentation requirement is not terribly onerous and is reasonable, the bulk of it being CV, transcripts, copies of your teaching qualifications and other documents you'd expect to have to include in a job search. Their fee is **£145 (US$225).** In comparison to other agencies, this fee is quite competitive, or at least it isn't unreasonable.

Also, if you are unsuccessful in a given recruiting season, the fee carries over so that you don't have to pay Search Associates for every year that you are on the job hunt. Your registration fee is good for up to three years.

Also, Search will hold your documentation pretty much indefinitely. I was searching for a new position in 2006 and arranged for the obligatory confidential reference letters. In 2016 when I was searching again, these documents were still in Search's database. At the Expat Teacher Network, we can only believe that this is a good thing. A variety of supportive references that span a wider time period is proof of your continued and consistent commitment to excellence in your profession. As is the case with many of the recruitment agencies (CIS, ISS, SCHROLE) these references can be requested with the proper forms directly via the applicable agency's website. As a candidate, it is not at all labour-intensive.

As previously mentioned, Search Associates holds a multitude of job fairs. Attendance at one job fair is included in the price of your sign-up fee. That means, your first fair is free! Not a bad deal. If you choose to attend multiple fairs, each additional fair costs only **US$75**. In the past, Search kept many of its fairs smaller, such that all candidates could be assured of landing at least some interviews. This admittedly makes the trip to the fair seem a lot more worthwhile.

However, in the interests of providing up-to-date information, we need to say that Search Associates has opted for a different market niche in the past 5 years or so. Their fairs, such as the January London fair have become very large – I guess with success comes size. The advantage to this is more schools and theoretically more jobs, and the benefits of 'conference rates' at hotels.

The disadvantage is the competition is obviously greater. At the 2016 London fair, which I attended, I noticed a lot of younger, UK-based teachers who were looking to go overseas for the first time. This was a distinct difference from my experience at earlier Search fairs and at the CIS London fair. All in all, Search fairs are well-run and attended by both good schools and good teachers. As a single person or a couple, you can go and have a decent chance of landing a job, or at least some interviews. Search claims to place over 3000 teachers per year – a claim that is certainly true. They also claim (or at least my senior associate does) that they place more teachers than all of the other recruitment agencies combined.

Search used to charge placement fees for candidates. When I got my job at my current school (Frankfurt) in 2000, I was charged US$600. These candidate placement fees are a thing of the past. Instead, Search Associates and other agencies have chosen to shift their fees to the schools. These fees are not cheap, but as a candidate they are obviously irrelevant to you.

d. **CIS/ECIS – Council of International Schools/European Council of International schools**
   www.cois.org

The next recruitment agency we want to discuss is the Council of International Schools, known as CIS. If you're a seasoned veteran of international schools, you've probably at some point in your career attended what used to be known as the ECIS

London Recruitment Fair. This fair was always held in the Marble Arch Hotel in London in January. We freely admit that in the course of our research for this guide, finding information about CIS and ECIS was difficult. So, we are forced to mention that in spite of the fact that we try very hard to present information in this guide that is up-to-date, this particular subsection is the one where the potential for inaccuracy is the highest. We are eager to hear of any errors or omissions so that we might offer the most accurate information possible to our members.

So the basic facts are: ECIS as an organization still exists but doesn't seem to be involved in recruitment anymore. This part of the business has passed to the newer CIS. This newer organization still conducts a London job fair, that is usually held on the weekend right before the Search London job fair. Therefore, if you were able to get a leave of absence or if mid to late-January happens to be a time when you normally get holidays at your school, attending both would be possible.

When it was still the ECIS London Recruitment Fair, this was the premiere job fair for many international schools. In the last 10 years, CIS and its recruitment efforts can really only be described by the phrase, "how the mighty have fallen". In spite of our attempts to learn, we can't even tell our readers and members for sure how big (or not) this fair currently is. What we _do_ know for sure is that many A-List schools no longer attend this far, for example my school (Frankfurt International School). When I asked my Head of School why not, his answer was simple: the quality of candidates at the Search Associates London fair was much better, such that attending both was a waste of the school's time and resources.

What's also true to say is that the CIS fair straddles the line between the selective and the non-selective type of fairs we mentioned earlier. They charge no fees to register and are happy to let you come to their fair – they took me in 1998 with only two years of teaching experience and no IB experience. However, no associate or otherwise helpful person is assigned to you and there is no "vetting" as there is with Search Associates. The upshot of all of this is: you could easily get to a CIS fair and you could just as easily find it a waste of time. There doesn't seem to be any screening of candidates. Attendance is done purely on a first-come-first-served basis. Therefore, there is no discussion or advice from their end as to whether attending this fair would be a good idea for a particular individual. So, in a sense, you are flying blind.

CIS also requires you to submit tons of documentation, which we would argue is unreasonable. This includes police clearances from every country you have ever lived in. This is probably what stops a lot of good, experienced teachers from registering with CIS. For me personally, even if I could get a police clearance from Ecuador, where I lived from August 1999 to June of 2000, what possible relevance could it have? Surely, if I have lived and worked in Germany for over 16 years a German police clearance is sufficient proof of my lack of criminal behavior.

The long and the short of it is, many schools seem to have switched their recruitment efforts away from CIS to Search Associates or to SCHROLE – more on them later. Having said that, if Europe or the Middle East is your target area and London is not a financially burdensome destination in terms of flights etc. AND if you are perhaps an experienced teacher but not so experienced with the IB Programme, perhaps CIS would be a job fair that you would consider.

As a final comment, CIS' website is easy enough to navigate, it is generally user-friendly but the disadvantage is unless you can provide the exhaustive amount of documentation they require, you will not be given access to their job vacancies. Also on occasion, our experience with their website is that it is not always technically reliable, though these technical problems were very few and far between.

e. ISS – International School Services
www.iss.edu

Our third and perhaps last of the globally-known recruitment agencies is ISS. This agency does more than just teacher recruitment. Their website shows clearly that ISS is not just a teacher recruitment agency anymore; they are also heavily into the business of educational consulting and school management.

The next, most important thing to say about ISS is that they are much more US-based and oriented than other recruitment agencies. While this isn't a disadvantage in and of itself, when registering, we personally found it a bit confusing sometimes that their online forms and lexicon assumed that their candidates were American.

ISS charges no placement fees but does charge a registration fee of **US$195**. ISS makes most of their profits from the membership fees they charge schools. My Head of School informed me that currently, these fees are US$12,000! This of course has a deterrent effect on many schools who prefer to work through other, less expensive agencies.

The documentation ISS demands of candidates is reasonable, and their website is quite user-friendly and like Search Associates and CIS all of the pertinent documents can simply be uploaded. You don't need to bother with sending envelopes full of copies of important documents and the long waits that this would mean. You can complete your profile quite quickly. Payment is also probably the most efficient of any of the various recruitment agencies. While Search Associates demands bank drafts sent to the Channel Islands or other various exotic banking locales, ISS allows you to pay via credit card, bank transfer or PayPal. This flexibility was welcome for me after having to go to my bank and arrange a wire transfer to the Channel Islands in order to re-activate my account with Search Associates.

Without question the most unique thing about ISS is their use of not only traditional face-to-face job fairs but also online fairs as well. They usually offer approximately 2-3 online fairs per recruiting season, one in the fall, one early in the new year and one in the spring (often in May). Candidates register for the fair and then indicate interest by joining a "chat queue" just as you might do if you were standing in line waiting to speak to a recruiter at a traditional job fair. Then, when your turn comes up, a chat window is opened and you can try to charm your way into a Skype interview with prospective recruiters. We freely admit, we have to date no experience with an online job fair nor do we know anyone who does. However, some obvious advantages and disadvantages come to mind.

1. If you use an online fair, you can save yourself the cost of airfare and hotels and meals out.
2. The online fair has to be held simultaneously for you and the recruiter, such that you might end up needing to be online at 3 a.m. or some other inconvenient hour due to the difference in time zones.
3. If your internet connection goes out – not an uncommon occurrence if you live in the developing world – then your participation in the fair is going to come to an abrupt halt. This obviously won't go down well with prospective recruiters.

ISS job fairs are large and are generally non-selective. This means you'll see a real mixture of lesser-experienced and more experienced candidates. Based on their website, ISS tends to attract a lot of schools from Latin America to their job fairs, so if this region is your target, then one of their fairs might be your best option.

ISS generally holds 3 online fairs and 3 traditional fairs per recruiting season. With the exception of their January fair in Bangkok, Thailand, all of these fairs are held in the US.

The downside to ISS job fairs is their size and the resulting consequences. Because they have such a large number of candidates, many A-List schools choose not to attend ISS fairs or they simply don't use ISS at all. My school (Frankfurt) still pays its fees to belong to ISS but it often does not attend an ISS fair. The reason is simple: given the large number of CVs a recruiter has to plow through to find the best, most-qualified candidates, an ISS fair is not the most cost-effective use of a recruiter's time if they are from an A-List school. The knock-on effect of this is that many candidates don't bother registering with ISS. A colleague of mine said simply, "I took a look at which schools attended their fairs, and decided I was better off saving myself the US$195." I freely admit, I am a registered candidate with ISS, but this is mainly only for research purposes for this guide and to be able to provide the most accurate information to Expat Teacher Network members. Otherwise, I also probably would not bother with ISS. If I were a lesser-experienced teacher, I might think differently.

The weakest link in ISS' chain is undoubtedly their job vacancies database. Every recruitment agency will allow you to access their jobs database once you are a fully paid-up active candidate. ISS has a decent database in terms of quantity. Their website allows you to browse the vacancies easily and they even have a quick "apply for this job" button that is very convenient and automatically indicates your interest to that school and sends them your information without you having to compose your own cover letter.

However, the jobs listed are notoriously out of date. One colleague at my school who was actually hired through ISS said he found this to be the most frustrating part of dealing with ISS. However, given his then-lack of international experience, Search Associates refused to take him, even though he had over 20 years of teaching experience! So, ISS proved to be a valuable tool for him and today he is a successful and contributing member of my school's faculty. My own experience with ISS' database confirms my colleague's experience. In 2016 I applied for a position at the

International School of Kenya in Nairobi. I did so directly and through Search Associates, as that was where the job was originally posted. I received many weeks later an "oh by the way" email notice from ISS informing me of the vacancy and that they had forwarded my documents to IS Kenya. This would normally be a terrific service, except that I knew from direct contact with the school and via the Search Associates Jobs Database that the position had long since been filled and was no longer open. Needless to say, such inaccuracies can be very frustrating and time-wasting when you're looking for a job.

As a final note, from a technical point of view, ISS' website is fine and functions well.

f. SCHROLE
www.schrole.com

Our next entry in this section is SCHROLE which is a rather unique animal really. Unlike the other agencies we've discussed up to this point, SCHROLE (no, I don't know what it stands for) is not really a recruitment agency in the traditional sense. They operate no job fairs, and offer little or no assistance to candidates. Really, Australian-based SCHROLE is just an internet portal/software platform that schools use to process applications for specific vacancies. Schools that use SCHROLE seem to be locked into an exclusive contract. If you notice a vacancy at a SCHROLE school and you try to contact the school directly, you will be asked to apply via the SCHROLE website. It does not cost to register with SCHROLE or to set up a profile – which is the better description of what you do – but they do have a "premium membership" that does cost. We have never bothered to pay for the premium membership at SCHROLE and so we cannot share what it entails. When you set up a profile with SCHROLE, the paperwork is not onerous. It's the usual documents you have to upload. There are also some general profile questions that you will be asked to answer.

What we at the Expat Teacher Network can say is that we have used SCHROLE to apply for a few jobs and it has never even led to an interview. Each school can set up its own questions in addition to the general questions that SCHROLE makes you answer when you set up your profile. In some mysterious way, this leads to "SCHROLE ratings". I know this from personal experience. I applied for a job at a SCHROLE school in the Middle East. I was not even contacted nor was I approached in any way. A friend of mine who works at the school investigated for me and was told my SCHROLE ratings were not good enough.

I admit, I didn't and don't know what this means. I tried investigating this, so as to be able to improve my ratings the next time a SCHROLE vacancy became available. I could find no answers, including from SCHROLE themselves as to what makes up their ratings or their rating system. Insofar as I can figure out, your SCHROLE profile consists mainly of objective data like nationality, teaching experience, subjects taught etc. In other words, data you can't really alter even if you wanted to. Needless to say, the whole experience was quite frustrating. I admit, I have always wondered if my lack of premium (ie. paid) membership played a role in my ratings. I decided to contact the principal of the school directly to ask him why I had not been contacted for an interview. Over the course of 3 months, he gave me three different answers.

Needless to say, I felt rather like the real truth was being kept from me. I have now removed this school from my list of places I am willing to apply to.

SCHROLE works differently as we have said. Basically, once you have set up your profile, you can search through SCHROLE's list of schools and "tag" the schools you think you would like to work for and when a vacancy at any of these schools comes up, SCHROLE will notify you. The problem with such a system is, SCHROLE doesn't seem to take your subjects/teachable areas into account. I routinely get SCHROLE notices in my profile for math jobs and other positions for which I am completely unqualified.

SCHROLE allows you to update your answers to your school-specific questions at any time, though obviously if the position is already filled, this is a waste of time. SCHROLE's website is for the most part technically reliable. The real downside is, you can't get around SCHROLE if the school you're applying to uses them. An increasing number of schools from the Middle East and Asia, including many A-List schools, are using SCHROLE. Their job postings are current, unlike some other agencies that we have already mentioned.

g. **TIE Online – The International Educator and TES – The Times Educational Supplement**
www.tieonline.com, www.tes.co.uk

Last but not least we come to two of the old stand-by sources for international teaching jobs. The International Educator newspaper has for many years been the international school standard for information dissemination. They used to have job postings in their hard-copy version. They may well still do this, but I admit I have not subscribed to TIE in a long time, so I don't know. What is clear, is that TIE has long-since moved their jobs database to their website. TIE used to be notorious for having job postings that were out of date. In theory this has improved since their database has moved online but was is still true, is that you will need to purchase a subscription to TIE in order to be able to view their vacancies. This leads us to the inescapable conclusion that not many schools and/or teachers still use TIE as their main method of recruitment.

By contrast, the job postings of the Times Educational Supplement (TES) out of the UK are current, accessible by anyone with an internet connection and the TES website is easy to use and seems to be technically sound. There is even a convenient "apply for this job" button on each of the postings, just as you would expect to find on the websites of the more mainstream recruitment agencies like Search Associates or ISS. TES contains mainly UK-Curriculum overseas schools as well as schools in the UK itself. If you don't have "National Curriculum" experience, you may find the number of jobs you can apply for is much more limited than with other agencies that are more geared towards non-nation-specific international schools. I have used TES myself and have had mixed results in terms of it leading to interviews. You can even set up a profile for free and arrange for email alerts for jobs for which you are qualified so that you don't need to be visiting their website constantly. The job postings have a search function (this is the industry norm) and the website is very user-friendly in general terms. If you're a UK-qualified teacher, especially if you have both IB and A-Level experience, TES can be a very useful tool.

Let's move on now to the other tools that are necessary for securing a job in international schools these days. Some will be obvious, some perhaps not. Without them, you do yourself a great disservice.

NOTES

6. International Schools, assessing them

Part SIX: International Schools: how can I find out more information about schools I have applied to?

As recently as 15 years ago, it was not really possible to find out much information about any particular school you had applied to. In a real sense, teachers applying to teach in international or overseas schools were really flying blind. Fortunately for prospective expat teachers, this has changed.

While there are certainly a multitude of blogs, websites and other places where a teacher can inform themselves – via the Expat Teacher Network is a good way – the most established portal through which an expatriate educator can inform themselves is ISR (International Schools Review) www.internationalschoolsreview.com. ISR is not a recruitment agency like the other organizations we have profiled thus far. ISR exists to allow educators a platform to exchange information about schools anonymously. ISR has a very comprehensive platform containing virtually every overseas school there is. Its website is not the most visually appealing in our opinion, but it functions properly and is generally user-friendly.

It should be mentioned that although ISR is a very valuable tool for educators, it must be used with caution. Anyone can pay the annual **US$29** fee and write a review. Reviews on ISR can be general reviews of a school or specific reviews of a particular administrator. There isn't any method that ISR uses to check to see if the writer is genuinely from that school or is genuinely a teacher and not an administrator. There are schools on ISR that have completely contradictory reviews. Generally speaking, the assumption by most colleagues we have spoken to, is that the glowing reports will have been written by a member of the administration who is worried the school's (and by extension their) reputation will be ruined.

Every school has its positives and negatives. What is also true is that international educators have to be flexible and willing to accept that international schools generally don't fall within the realm of a higher educational authority. This means that their curriculum, focus, mission and philosophy are up for discussion or at least must be decided in house. This can be frustrating for many people who have a highly developed sense of their own educational philosophy. Dealing with colleagues who have a philosophy that stands in direct contradiction to your own can be hard.

We do not therefore wish to say that a school with one negative review on ISR should have its reputation forever sullied. But, a pattern of negative reviews is definitely a warning sign that experienced educators will do well to heed. At my last job fair, I was offered a job by a school in Dhahran, Saudi Arabia. I found the note in my file on the second morning of the job fair. Fortunately, I had my laptop with me and there was WiFi in the hotel. I immediately got on ISR and found a pattern of not only negative, but scathing reviews of the school I had interviewed with. Needless to say, I sent them a polite, "thanks but no thanks" note.

ISR can be tricky though. Some schools can have both positive and negative reviews. After all, this is the case with my own school (Frankfurt) if you research it on ISR. Sometimes this is the result of a particularly difficult colleague, other times the reasons are more straight-forward. The usual reason for this is a change in the school's management. In our assessment, the key to assessing an ISR review can be boiled down to two factors you MUST keep in mind:

1. Are the ISR reviews of this school repetitively negative or positive?
2. When were the reviews written?

Number 2 can be really key. Nearly all of the negative comments about my own school on ISR stem from the tenure of the former headmaster. He has been gone for six years now and to be as objective as possible, the school is not the same place. Heads of School, Directors, Superintendents, whatever name a school's boss may go by, they do influence the atmosphere of a school to a large extent. Our main point here is this: if the negative reviews are a few years old and you check the school's website and discover that there is a new Head of School and/or a new Principal, you need to take the negative review with a grain of salt. Things could very well be different in the present day.

This is our take on ISR. Many colleagues, including administrators find it valuable. After all, they sometimes look for jobs too! With such a low annual cost, it is difficult to pass up such a valuable service.

NOTES

41

7. Effective Job Search Tips from the Experts

Part SEVEN: What other tools do I need to be successful in my job search?

Now that we've covered job fairs, recruitment agencies, ISR, Emails and teaching portfolios, what other tools does a teacher need these days in order to have the best chance of landing a job at an international school?

Again, the advice-giver websites can be very long-winded about such things. We've tried to boil it down for our members and to stick once again to items that are generally agreed upon or simply verifiable facts. Insofar as we can ascertain, in addition to the basic requirements (certification, experience, a CV, decent interview skills), you absolutely need to have these two tools: a Skype account and your own webpage.

I. Skype Accounts for video calls:

You've almost certainly heard of or used Skype unless you've been living under a large rock for the last ten years, or you're tech-phobic enough that you don't even own a computer and don't surf the internet - yes, there really are people out there like this, although granted, usually they are retirees, not searching for employment. Or if they are active teachers searching for employment, they have a steep learning curve ahead.

Downloading and installing Skype onto your computer is free and easy. Skype has been around long enough that getting your plain name as your Skype user name will be virtually impossible now. It's the same reason why many people have a Hotmail or Gmail account with a slew of numbers included in their user name. Skype is no different. No matter, as long as you put your Skype account user name on your CV and on your personal webpage, you'll be fine.

Some of the advice-giver websites say that Skype is "highly recommended" - I think this is the exact phrasing that Search Associates uses when you register with them. At the Expat Teacher Network, we would be willing to go even further. If you don't have Skype, you're screwed. Blunt language yes, but true.

The fact of the matter is, schools use Skype liberally these days to help cut down on their recruiting costs. Flying administrators all over the world to job fairs, which involves hotel costs, meals, flights, is expensive. Teachers who attend these job fairs know this better than anyone. Skype has become the industry standard for "alternative" interviews. At my school, I am losing count as to how many colleagues had a Skype interview as part of their hiring process. So, if you don't have a Skype account, for whatever reason, we advise you to get one. Again, if you don't have Skype, you're screwed.

If you have one, but the user name is not professional for whatever reason, sign up for another Skype account with a name that is more conducive to professional contacts. For example, I have a former colleague whose email address is very close to unionizenowteacher@xxyyzz.com (sorry, I will not ACTUALLY share someone's private email in a public document, it's the user name that's important anyway, not the provider). She is a union negotiator and a passionate believer in workers' rights and equality. I admire her for this. She has been helpful to me personally with information when I became a union negotiator at my school. But it's probably not the best email address to use in a job search. Personally, my history as a union rep is NOT something I share with prospective employers. I will not lie if they ask, but I don't offer.

Optional: Effective Skype Interviews

There are a couple of dos and don'ts when it comes to interviewing via Skype. We'll take a brief moment to talk about them too. Granted, perhaps this does not quite fit into the whole philosophy behind this guide, but these dos and don'ts are not necessarily intuitive or obvious, especially to the technically-challenged (a group we readily put ourselves into as well, by the way).

The easiest way to deal with this is via a numbered list of Five Key Points. The list makes one rather large assumption: that your internet connection is stable, fast and reliable. If it's not, you need to find one that is. Either at your school/office or at a friend's home. Not an internet cafe or other public place. These are noisy, and most importantly, not private.

1. **Ensure you have a good setup.**

   This is crucial - as bad lighting can make you look pale, sickly or is just generally a bad representation of yourself. Just like a real interview, it's common sense that you're trying to make a good impression. If the recruiter can see you properly, this is a big help in making that positive impression. The interview will probably be recorded.

   Do a practice call with a friend before the real interview, if you're not sure if your lighting is good, and ask them if you look like you. Don't be afraid to ask someone for help in getting your lighting done right. Make sure you eliminate any glare that will interfere with your video depiction. In the JoyJobs Guide they mention turning the sharpness down to two or three to produce softer skin tones.[3] This is probably good advice.

   Some advice-givers will suggest putting up a blank screen behind you. This seems to be a bit of overkill. After all, is it so bad if your prospective employer sees you sitting in front of a shelf full of books? Doesn't this add credibility to your academic standing? If it is such a bad background, why is it used so often by professional journalists? You want to look professional in a professional setting – it would be worth your while to do so.

2. **Be in a quiet location and make sure you won't be disturbed.**

---

[3] ibid., p. 55.

This is code for <u>turn off your mobile phone</u>! Unplug the landline if you have one. Close the door to the room, and don't leave the window open such that street noise can interfere with your interview. Notify everyone of the importance of the call and make sure you are undisturbed. Better yet, tell them to get lost and take the dog with them.

3. **Make sure your sound is good.**

If your Skype interview loses video, it is not the end of the world. After all, the two of you can still talk and ask each other questions.

If audio goes, however, the interview is over. Even though it might not be your fault, this doesn't bode well if it happens.

The easiest way around this is to make sure you have a good connection and as we've already suggested, do a practice call with a friend about 15-30 minutes before your interview and have them tell you if your setup is good. You can't really know what you and your Skype look like from the other end. One two-minute Skype call to a friend or family member, preferably someone in another country will be a good test of how well your Skype is working at that moment.

It helps to have a microphone or cell phone mic handy in case.

4. **Arrange a comfortable time.**

I once did a professional development course based in the US. I live in Central Europe. The course ran at 3 a.m. my time and I had to get up and go to school the next day. Not good. Don't make this mistake with a Skype interview for a prospective job. Make sure the time is a <u>convenient one for you</u>. You don't want to be rushed. You'll probably be anxious enough. Don't be afraid to insist on a time that is convenient for both you and the school. If they refuse, move on.

5. **Interview professionally and seriously.**

So, what this means is simple: dress appropriately, don't wear ratty old clothes. Wear the complete outfit, including shoes, after having a shower – we shouldn't have to mention this but you would be surprised how many people think you can do a skype interview in shorts… Have your student work ready to flash at the interviewer. Treat the interview as if it were a real one. Because it is.

Ask questions, prepare them ahead of time if you need to and above all, take notes. Noting down information and answers from a Director indicates you're serious about the position. Obviously schools like that.

Those are the basics of a Skype interview in as succinct a manner as we can put it. Let's move on to the second tool no international job-seeking teacher should be without these days, a <u>personal website</u>.

II. Personal Websites

Ironically, the greatest advantage of the internet is its greatest danger: anyone can get on it. While this means we live in a world where we are forced to police more heavily what our young people are exposed to in terms of video and written content, the positive side is anyone can build a website and unlike the early days of the internet, you can do so without any knowledge of HTML programming. I am living proof of this. I run four different websites, own five different domain names and I have never studied HTML in my life and have no clue about it.

Some advice-givers, like JoyJobs will offer personal websites as part of their membership services. Naturally, you have to pay for their memberships, but it is a pretty good value, all things considered. What really seems to be the industry standard these days, is an account on LinkedIn. For whatever reason (probably because they were first or nearly first) LinkedIn has become the main social networking site for professionals, teachers included. The advantage to LinkedIn, or even to free webhosting services like Weebly, or Wordpress, is obvious: you don't have to pay. The downside is that you need to know more about webpage creation.

With the services that will do it for you, you simply send them your information, and presto, you have your own webpage. At JoyJobs for example, they have even configured the webpage such that a recruiter only has to click on the "Skype me" button and it will open their Skype software and begin to ring you. On a self-made webpage, you can't always include such things. So, you have to decide how important it is to you to have this feature.

Here at Expat Teacher Network, we're a bit undecided on that one. A Head of School who can't open his/her own Skype and add you to their contacts and then call you, is probably someone you shouldn't seriously consider working for. Plus, if you have your own self-made webpage, you can choose the colour scheme and many other features yourself.

Another advantage to the self-made webpage, is you can update it instantly. With the pre-fab pages like JoyJobs, you have no say or choice in regard to colour scheme or how fast your new photos, information and documents will be uploaded and available to recruiters. I myself started with a JoyJobs website and quickly decided I was better off on my own. We've tried to boil down the key dos and don'ts of making a personal website it into a list.

- **Include a high quality teacher professional photo.** It may be fun to include a photo of yourself in a more relaxed situation, but it can make the wrong impression. Passport photos are no longer any good of course, because they need to be biometric and are too serious looking.

- **Use a clear, easy-to-read font.** Fancy fonts can be fun or even desirable for your home business or some other situation, but hunting for a job as a teacher at an international school needs to be plainer and more "boring" or put another way, it needs to be accessible and professional and won't raise any red flags for the parents of your future students.

- **Use an easy-to-view text to background colour combination.** Believe it or not, basic black on yellow or white is the easiest for the human eye to digest. Fancy colours only make your text more difficult to see. See an example below of a simple black on yellow colour scheme, complete with the important links we mention below.

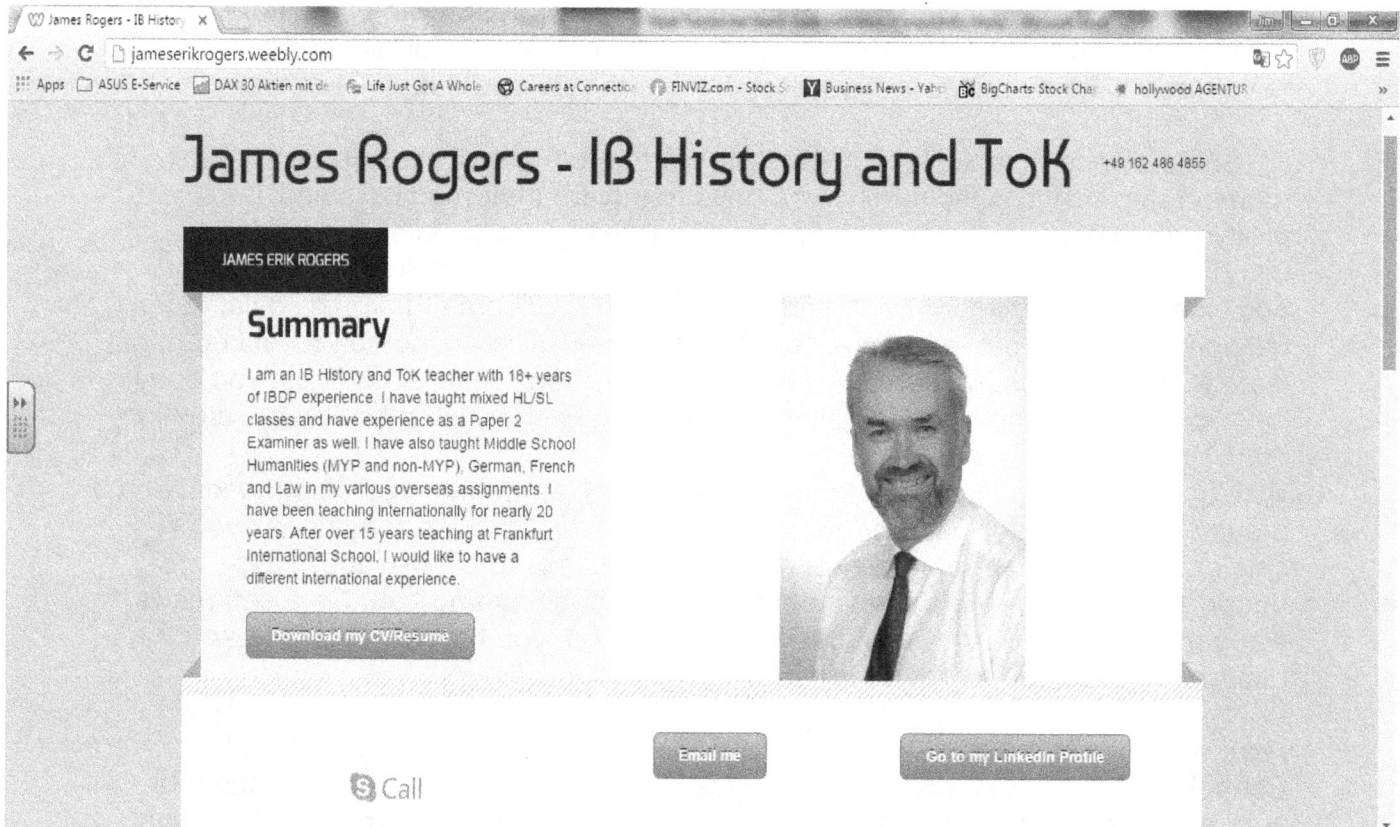

- **Include a link to download your resumé/CV.** Your personal webpage and/or your LinkedIn profile **MUST** include a button that automatically downloads your CV in PDF format. Without this, your important data is not accessible enough. This puts you at a great disadvantage.

- **Include a link to your LinkedIn profile.** LinkedIn has really become the place where other professionals will expect you to have a profile. Not having one again, puts you at a disadvantage. Creating a profile is free of charge, so there's no reason not to.

- **Include a link to your Skype address or display your Skype ID prominently.** Some of the paid services, like JoyJobs, offer to build you a webpage that has a convenient button where a visitor can click on it, and it automatically opens their Skype and calls you. If you build your own webpage with a free hosting service, you can embed your own Skype call button, simply by visiting the "Skype buttons" page of the "features" part of Skype's own website. It is incredibly easy and takes only a few moments.

You type in your Skype Name, make sure the "call" option is checked and choose the size of the Skype button you wish to include and voila, you get the embed code for your Skype button. We've taken a screen shot of the appropriate page on the Skype website, so you can see what it looks like. Once you have your embed code, you simply need to click on the "embed code" button in your sitebuilder software and copy and paste the code into the box. Below is a screenshot of how I did mine. I use Weebly as my sitebuilder for my personal webpage. I have never known a sitebuilder software that didn't have an option to embed HTML code.

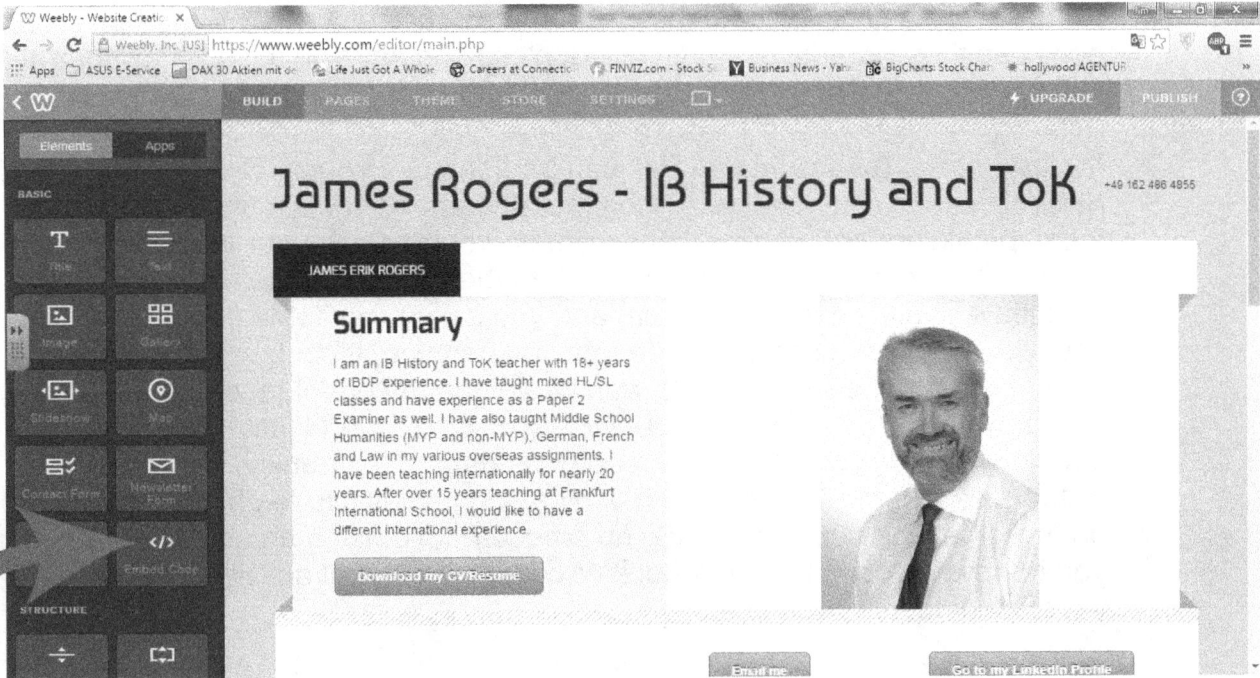

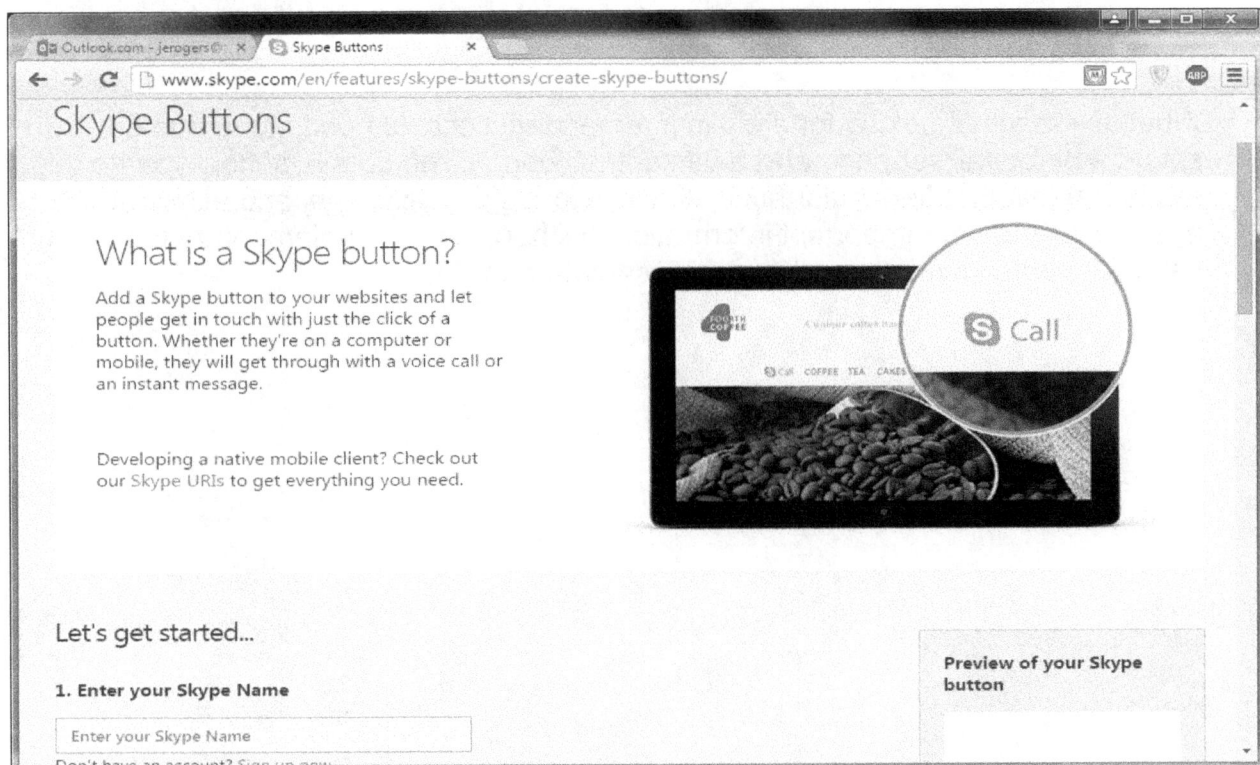

- **Include a link to your email.** Schools that cannot contact you simply by email will, to put it bluntly, move on to the next candidate.

- **Include a summary of your experience and qualifications.** After all, as we've already mentioned, your experience and qualifications will be the key to getting noticed by schools and it is what makes you the needle and not just part of the haystack.

- **Include a personal statement about your teaching philosophy.** The key here is to be honest, but not aggressive. If you believe in consistent assessment, say so. If you think programmes such as the MYP are horrible, don't use those words, but definitely don't lie and say you think it's wonderful just to get hired. Remember, the key is to find the *right* job, not just any job.

- **Include some testimonials.** This can be done in a couple of ways. Either you have access to your letters of recommendation and you simply quote from them, providing "sound bites" that promote yourself and your teaching, or you don't have access (many reference letters these days are confidential, ie. the candidate doesn't get to see them) and you ask any suitable person to provide you with a 2-3 sentence quotation that you can use. It could be argued, it's better if it's not the same people who wrote your letters of recommendation, as it shows your abilities are more widely respected than just those few people who provided you with a recommendation, but frankly, we don't think this makes much difference. Both Janice and I also include photos of students doing something such as holding up a poster advertising an event you ran, or you holding a copy of the yearbook or coaching student activities as long as you cannot identify students.

So, that's our take on personal webpages. We mentioned LinkedIn, but we didn't talk about it much because it uses a pre-done format to a large extent and it is easy and self-explanatory.

What any teacher looking for a job in international schools needs to remember is to set up a personal webpage **and** a LinkedIn account. The details of how you do this are less relevant. Most importantly, it needs to <u>look professional</u> and allow recruiters <u>easy access</u> to your important information. Without these supplementary tools, any candidate puts themselves at a great disadvantage.

NOTES

8. Final Thoughts for Successful Job Hunting

The key to landing an international school job that is right for you is to understand that the process is a two-way street. The more experience and qualifications you have, the truer this is.

I have experienced interviews with Directors that were, to be frank, arrogant. Their whole approach to the interview was one of "<u>What makes you think you're good enough to work at my school</u>?" This is definitely a danger sign and one that any candidate would do well to heed. It is a good sign if a Director is proud of his/her school. After all, the opposite would be seriously worrying.

However, like many times when pride, dignity and self-confidence are involved, there's a limit to what is reasonable. It is legitimate for Heads of School to want to hire the best available candidates.

It is also legitimate for candidates to want to work for the best available schools. In other words, it's not just a matter of "Are you good enough to work at my school?", it is also a matter of "<u>Is your school good enough that they deserve a terrific teacher like me?</u>".

The important factor to remember is you are not just being interviewed, you are also doing the interviewing. The school has to be the <u>right fit for you</u> too, not just the other way around. Figuring this out can be very challenging. There are a multitude of factors for a teacher to consider. Some, not all, we have listed here:

- Is the school offering a <u>one or two year contract</u>?
- Is the <u>contract renewable</u>?
- If you decide to stay, are there <u>residency limits</u> imposed on foreigners in the host country?
- Are <u>extra-curricular activities mandatory</u> or voluntary?
- If they are voluntary, and you choose not to participate, will this affect your <u>future employment</u>?
- What is the <u>mandatory meeting schedule</u> and is it reasonable?
- How long is the <u>normal school day</u>?
- How <u>many days</u> is a teacher expected to work in a given school year?
- What is your <u>teaching assignment</u> going to be? Can the Director even answer this question definitively?
- Will you have your <u>own classroom</u> or will you have to teach in different rooms?
- What is the school's policy/response to <u>discipline issues</u>?

- What is the <u>composition of the student body</u>? How many are expatriates and how many are locals?
- Does the school have a <u>salary scale</u>? If not, why not?
- What is the <u>normal cost of living</u> (rent, electricity, heat/AC, food, etc.) in the host country?
- How much can a teacher/teaching couple <u>realistically save</u> in a month/year?
- In what <u>currency</u> is your salary paid? Is it easily convertible and transferable out of the country?
- What opportunities, if any, are there for a teacher/teaching couple to have a <u>social life</u> outside of school?

Hopefully by now you feel better informed and ready to dive into the world of international teaching. If you've already taken the plunge, you feel like your decision was a good one.

Here at the Expat Teacher Network, we don't pretend to know everything. There are certainly items that we have forgotten to include, or that can be found in other sources, but not here. One of our goals was to keep this guide relatively succinct in order to make it more accessible to our members. Contact us directly via our website or Fiverr to connect with your queries.

Whether you're already addicted to the expat teacher lifestyle, or hoping to become hooked, we wish you the best of luck in the classroom and the best of adventures.

NOTES

About The Authors

JAMES ROGERS has been an international educator on 4 continents for over 20 years. A graduate in History and German, since 1998 James has taught IB DP History, Theory of Knowledge and ITGS (Information Technology in a Global Society). In addition, he has been an IB History Paper 2 Examiner as well.

James Rogers has written both editions of The Expat Teacher Job Search Guide and is the founder of the Expat Teacher Network http://expatteachernetwork.com/index.html.

JANICE SETO
With a background in sales, marketing, hospitality, labour relations, and consulting in human performance, and international education, Janice Seto writes on a variety of issues and is a member of the American Psychological Association's Community College division, the Yoga Alliance and the International Enneagram Association. She is a contributing author to James Rogers's The Expat Teacher Job Search Guide, the original edition and the second edition.

Janice and James have been friends since they taught together at a Canadian curriculum school in Malaysia. Currently, Janice divides her time between her hometown Bowmanville and various airports.

Her latest books include *Johnny Seto's Bowmanville An Enneagram Perspective*, the sequel to *Johnny's Place: The Coronation Restaurant* and *Segovia Restaurant: Espana in Toronto by Ino* and *Get Yourself a Classroom: How Smart Canadian Teachers Land Fulltime Jobs in Tough Times*.

Inquiries should be addressed to Janice(dot)seto(at)me.com
Janice Seto's websites http://www.janiceseto.com and http://janiceseto.wix.com/words

www.ingramcontent.com/pod-product-compliance
Lightning Source LLC
Chambersburg PA
CBHW051426200326

41520CB00023B/7369

9 781926 935171